OKI'S ISLAND

a hero's journey

KENNY KEMP

Designed by Bonnie Sheets
Interior images by Kenny Kemp

Library of Congress Cataloging-in-Publication Data

Kemp, Kenny.

 Oki's island : a hero's journey / by Kenny Kemp.

    p. cm.

 ISBN-13: 978-1-892442-35-2 (hardback : alk. paper)

 ISBN-10: 1-892442-35-3 (hardback : alk. paper)

 1. Fishers--Fiction. 2. Polynesia--Fiction. I. Title.

 PS3561.E39922O35 2006

 813'.54--dc22   2006001761

02   03   04   05

for Bill and Lisa,
welcome fellow travelers

one

Oki hurled the net high into the azure sky. It fell on the gently rolling sea and slowly sank. In the clear turquoise water, he could see the fish darting away from the sinking net. Most would escape, but he would haul a few on board his small outrigger, to feed the hungry celebrants at tomorrow's great feast following the yearly Ritual.

As he pulled the net into the boat, he looked back over his shoulder. There on the white horizon, well within an hour's steady paddling, rose the lush green hills of his island home. Coconut palms dotted white beaches, and waterfall threads glistened against the towering volcano, tendrils of gray smoke rising from its pinnacle, a constant reminder that Oki and his people lived on a knife-edge.

Pulling the fish out of his net and placing them into the woven baskets, Oki thought about the upcoming Ritual. Tomorrow night, the villagers would stand on one side of the common area, and the sixteen young virgins on the other, dressed in their whitest *kalas*, their long black hair glistening in the torchlight, their eyes excited and fearful. The witch-doctor would stand between the two groups and utter the ancient prayers. All would bow their heads and listen to the distant rumbling of the volcano, high above them. Then the witch-doctor would lead the procession up the stony path toward the volcano summit. No one would utter a sound and only the wind in the palms and the muffled roar of the surf on the beach would be heard. At the summit, the witch-doctor would listen to the silent voice of God and one girl would be chosen to appease His anger at the people's sins. Satisfied by the virgin sacrifice, God would then guide the terrible hurricanes away from their tiny island for another year.

And after the sacrifice, they would descend the steep, rocky path rejoicing, beating their log drums and piping their bamboo flutes, their voices loud enough for God himself to hear, and the yearly feast would begin. Oki would spear his fish on the spit and turn them slowly over the crackling fire. Sweet coconut milk would flow, and the rich, fatty smell of roast pig would fill the sultry air. Turtle shells of ripe mangos, papaya, passion fruit, and pineapple would be passed around, and streams of fruit juice would dribble from smiling mouths as the people danced and celebrated their good fortune and hopes for another peaceful and prosperous year.

Oki had his own small part in the Ritual, and he was delighted to see his net coming up fuller than usual. Surely God had been pleased at his prayer this morning as he cast off. "I dedicate my catch to You," he'd whispered as he pushed his outrigger into the lagoon. "May it sharpen Your love and blunt Your anger toward us, Your only children."

Yet even as he pulled the last shining fish from the net, Oki heard distant thunder. He looked back at the island, expecting to see flashes of fire erupting from the volcano summit. Instead, he saw a great bank of black clouds behind the island, rushing toward him. Almost immediately he felt the push of cold wind against his bare chest, and lightning forked onto the island an instant before black clouds obscured it entirely.

Oki held his net loosely in his hands, his heart racing. One moment he was drifting on the gently rolling waters within a short paddle of the only land he'd ever known, and the next he was clutching the gunwales as his tiny craft was tossed about on immense waves. As he crested a towering swell, he looked back again. The island was gone, as was the sun, which had shone warm just moments before. Then he was hurled into a deep trough, and a gigantic wave broke overhead, filling his outrigger with water.

The baskets overturned and the fish flopped about in the boat's keel. Oki bailed and prayed, not daring to look up, feeling, rather than seeing, the onrush of the next immense swell. Cresting the wave, he looked about. All was dark, the sun was no more, and rain began to fall from the sky in icy sheets.

Oki dropped the bailing bucket and cried out in fear. "What have I done, God?" he pleaded, his hands clasped together and his eyes shut against the storm, his tears mingling with the salt spray. A moment before he collapsed into weary exhaustion, he thought, *Is the ocean nothing more than men's tears?*

 **TWO**

a small fish brushed against his cheek, startling Oki awake. He looked up. The sky was a deep, familiar blue. He sat up and looked around. In every direction, empty sea met empty sky. His island was nowhere in sight.

He began bailing his outrigger, which, though it was full of water, had survived the storm with little damage. One of the riggers was loose, so he cut off a corner of his net and lashed the rigger securely onto the spar. The ocean rolled quietly, as if it was just another day. But for Oki, the storm had just begun. His island! He had no idea in which direction it lay. Night would come shortly, and though Oki knew the

North Star, he did not know whether he was north or south of his island. If he followed it, it might lead him even farther away from land.

Having been raised on a small island—the *only* island in a world of endless seas—he was used to fearing the expanse of ocean which surrounded it. Throughout his life he had heard stories around the fire pit about unwary fishermen or foolish explorers who had lost sight of land, never to return. Oki had shivered even in the warmth of the fire, knowing that he must always keep the island in sight as he fished, for God would not save him if he broke that cardinal commandment.

"It is for our protection," said the witch-doctor. "God warns us to stay close to home. If we are disobedient, we will suffer His wrath."

Oki scanned the horizon. He must have been disobedient—but what had he done? He obeyed the witch-doctor's commandments and honored the holy days. His own sister had been offered up to God three years ago, and though he had seen the fear and anguish in her eyes, he knew it was God's will that she represent the people in the Ritual.

He racked his brain, cataloging his sins, which though minor, were nevertheless numerous. He was guilty of occasionally taking more than his fair share of food, or of forgetting to wash himself before sleep, and once he had even chewed the forbidden *bukari root*, which brought on a pleasant, dull stupor. But he had expiated his sin by receiving a single flog from the witch-doctor with the spiky scepter.

"If you had not confessed, you would have received another," said the witch-doctor, squeezing the aloe gel onto Oki's bloody cuts and gently working it in. "God will forgive you, if you promise to not do it again."

"I promise," said Oki, tears gathering at the corners of his eyes, his head bowed.

And he had kept his promise. So now, out here on the empty ocean, he lifted his eyes and prayed, asking what he had done to incur God's wrath.

But God did not answer Oki; He never did. All communications from God came to the witch-doctor. So it was not with much expectation that Oki prayed, and when the moment passed and God was silent,

Oki picked up his paddle. If God had cast him out for his wickedness, it really didn't matter what he had done; it was obviously bad enough to merit being lost at sea. All he could do now was paddle with all his might, keep his thoughts and hopes focused, and show God that he was repentant of the sin—whatever it was—that had merited his expulsion from the World.

Perhaps God would allow him to return if he proved himself worthy. Oki looked at the few remaining fish in the wicker basket. His net lay tangled in the bow of the boat. He still had his obsidian knife in its leather sheath at his waist. He would not starve. God had been kind enough to see to that. All was not lost. An opportunity had opened up before him. He could still prove himself worthy to join his people once more.

As the sun set, Oki paddled in the direction that seemed best. When the North Star appeared, he noted with satisfaction that he had already been rowing in that direction. He had been south of the island when the storm came up. Perhaps it still lay to the north. He chewed a piece of raw fish, his eyes never leaving the star. *I will return home,* he promised himself, dipping his paddle rhythmically into the glassy water.

THRee

For three days Oki paddled, because there was no wind. But on the afternoon of the third day, the wind began to blow again, and he lifted his small triangular sail. Using his paddle as a tiller, his heart lifted, for he felt in the wind at his back the warm breath of God.

Then, toward nightfall, he saw his island! The volcano rose high above the jungled slopes. The wind was pushing him straight for the island, and tears sprang from Oki's eyes as he thanked God.

Just beyond the atoll reef, the wind magically died, and Oki lowered the sail. Many huts stood on the beach inside the placid lagoon. He looked up at the volcano, expecting to see the great waterfall cascading down its lower slopes.

It was not there.

He looked for the familiar rock outcropping called God's Nose.

It was not there.

As he paddled across the lagoon, he looked for the lodge, big enough for fifty people.

It was not there.

Oki lifted his paddle and scanned the beach. There were many people working on the shore. Someone saw him and shouted, and soon everyone was looking at him. He glided onto the sand, scanning each face, but no one looked familiar. Yet they greeted him warmly, running to him and pulling him from his outrigger, slapping him on the back, smiling and laughing. They led him toward the common area which surrounded a great pit, in the center of which a bonfire leapt and crackled.

Oki looked around in dumb amazement. Who were these people? Could this be his island? No, there was only one village, one lagoon, one great waterfall, and one Nose of God. Yet they spoke his tongue, smiled like he was one of them, and handed him bowls of fruit and a large saucer of clear, sweet water.

Then the people parted and the witch-doctor appeared. He was older than the witch-doctor of Oki's island, and more fierce. His eyes burned from under the shadow of his parrot feather headdress, and he held a long staff, the head bristling with sharp palm spines, the tips of which were blackened with dried blood. "You have come across the deep waters," he said, pointing a bony finger at Oki.

Oki gulped and nodded.

"You have tested the wrath of God!" shouted the witch-doctor.

Oki hung his head and nodded again.

"And you have survived!" cried the witch-doctor.

Oki raised his head and looked around. The people were smiling. "It is a sign!" cried the witch-doctor as he lifted his scepter high over his head. "Tonight's Ritual will be accepted!"

Oki smiled. He had not missed it after all! God may have taken him to another island, but he had not missed the Ritual! Tears sprang to Oki's eyes as he joined the people standing on one side of the fire pit. Darkness came on and great, smoking torches were lit. Someone began chanting an unfamiliar song, and everyone closed their eyes. Oki shut his eyes as well, trying to sing along with the strange melody and odd words.

When they finished and Oki opened his eyes, he saw the sixteen young virgins standing on the other side of the fire, dressed in their whitest *kalas*. Their eyes shone with fear and excitement, as did the girls' eyes on Oki's island.

Oki breathed a sigh of relief. He had survived the ordeal and had been forgiven by God. He would worry about finding his own island tomorrow. Tonight, he would rejoice with this people—so very much like his own—as they offered sacrifice to quell

God's mighty anger and forestall the hurricanes and volcanic eruptions.

The witch-doctor led the procession up the mountain. The maw of the fiery volcano was even bigger than on Oki's island, and the lava below bubbled with great fierceness. Heat rose in great waves, and great gouts of steam wafted up, engulfing the villagers, who stood silently on the cauldron's lip.

The witch-doctor walked out onto the jutting precipice, lifted his hands heavenward, and prayed. Oki bowed his head. A peace settled over him. He was on an island much like his own, sharing the sacred Ritual with a people who were much like his own people. The witch-doctor finished his prayer and turned. He looked down the line of shivering girls. They were all crying, which surprised Oki. He wanted to comfort them, to tell them it would be over in a moment, and they would find peace. But as he stepped forward, hands grabbed his shoulders and pulled him back. The witch-doctor walked down the line of girls, surveying each one. Their terrified shrieks pierced Oki's heart. Something was wrong.

Didn't they know their sacrifice would bring God's blessings? Didn't they know they were *chosen*?

The witch-doctor stopped before a young girl, and the others ran back to their parents, who hugged them as if they had just returned from the dead. The chosen girl stood trembling, tears coursing down her cheeks. Oki saw a depth of terror in her eyes he had never seen before in any human being. "You are chosen," said the witch-doctor, taking the girl's hand and leading her out onto the precipice.

Oki looked for the witch-doctor's spiny scepter. It was held by a tall, broad-shouldered man, who stood with the other villagers. The witch-doctor began shouting a prayer to God. Oki looked back at the man with the scepter. *Give it to him!* he pleaded silently, but the man did not move. Then the witch-doctor turned and pointed at the people. "Why are we here?"

"To sacrifice!" they cried.

"Who shall we sacrifice?"

"Her!" shouted the people, pointing at the girl, who suddenly swooned in the witch-doctor's arms. He looked heavenward. "Thy will be done!"

Suddenly, Oki knew the Ritual had gone terribly wrong. "No!" he shouted, breaking free and rushing toward the precipice. But it was too late. The witch-doctor pushed the girl off the rocky shelf. She fell, screaming, into the volcano's fiery mouth. Oki fell at the witch-doctor's feet, crying, "No! No!"

Several men took hold of Oki, raising him up. The witch-doctor frowned. "You killed her!" shouted Oki, his eyes on the bubbling lava pool hundreds of feet below. The girl's body was gone. He looked up at the witch-doctor, hatred filling his eyes. "You killed her!"

"You assented to it, as did we all."

"I didn't know you were going to *kill* her!"

"How else would we offer sacrifice?" asked the witch-doctor, puzzled.

Oki broke free and grabbed the scepter from the strong man, shoving it into the witch-doctor's hands. "You're supposed to flog her, punish her for our sins. Then you rub aloe on her cuts and receive her back into fellowship. That's how it's done!"

"On *your* island," said the witch-doctor, frowning.

"Yes!" said Oki. "This is wrong!"

"And how do you know we're wrong?" asked the witch-doctor flatly.

"Your scepter! What do you think it's for?"

The witch-doctor looked the scepter over closely, examining the long, sharp spines coated with dried blood. Then he looked at Oki, darkness in his deep-set eyes.

"This? Why, it is for *you*."

 **FOUR**

Oki was shaken awake the next morning. When he tried to move, his back screamed in pain, and Oki screamed as well. One of the young virgins from the night before was standing before him, holding a shallow bowl. "You must not move," she said as she dipped a sponge. Oki felt the cool balm of aloe on his bloody cuts. "He gave you ten strokes," said the girl. "I've never seen anyone receive that many."

Oki tried to speak, but his tongue was swollen with thirst. The pain in his back was excruciating, but the girl's touch was light and soon she was done. "You will heal, traveler."

She left the small hut. Oki slowly got to his feet and stumbled out into the common area. All the villagers were there, forming two lines which led to the beach. He was meant to walk between the two rows. Oki started forward. The islander's faces were set, their eyes dark with hatred. He expected to be hit or kicked as he passed, but no one touched him. They did, however, spit upon him, scowling and yelling, calling him a devil, possessed with an evil spirit.

The witch-doctor stood on the shore of the lagoon. The people then formed a solid wall between Oki and the village, then turned their backs on him. Oki stood before the witch-doctor, wiping spit from his stinging eyes, his bloody back bowed in pain.

The witch-doctor took Oki's arm gently and led him to the outrigger, which was filled with coconuts, baskets of fruit, and gourds of fresh water. Surprised, Oki looked up into the face of the old man. "What is this?"

"You cannot stay," said the witch-doctor. "You would not be happy here."

Oki saw the truth in the old man's words. "And if I stayed, *you* would not be happy, either."

"We worship God as He has commanded."

Oki shook his head. "But you are wrong."

Surprise lit the witch-doctor's face. "Are *you* a witch-doctor? Do *you* know the mind of God?"

"No. I'm just a fisherman."

"A fisherman who is *lost*," amended the witch-doctor. "Lost because God is punishing you."

Oki nodded. It was the only possible answer.

"On your island, you only flog the girl?" whispered the witch-doctor.

Oki nodded.

"But isn't death a greater sacrifice than mere flogging—wouldn't it please God more?"

Oki did not know what to say. As the old man had pointed out, he was not a witch-doctor.

"I pray your people will find the greater truth," said the witch-doctor. He glanced at the villagers, who still stood with their backs to them. He leaned toward Oki and whispered, "For the safety of all, you must go."

Oki nodded and climbed into the outrigger. He picked up his paddle and stroked three times, then turned around. Everyone on the beach still had their backs to him. Only the girl who salved his wounds stood facing the lagoon, a puzzled look on her face.

 **FIVE**

all that morning, with each painful dip of his paddle, Oki rehearsed the events of the night before, comparing the two versions of the Ritual. On his island, the girl is flogged five times— a truly terrible ordeal, to be sure—but after, her wounds are treated. Her tears are collected in a bowl and cast into the volcano, and she is carried down the mountain as the people sing songs celebrating her sacrifice. She is placed in the seat of honor at the feast, and forever after, the scars on her back are a reminder to the people of the cost of disobedience. Throughout the following year, she is the only royalty the islanders know. Her food is brought to her; her body is washed reverently by the women, and the men look upon her with respect and honor. God forestalls the hurricanes and volcanic eruptions, and the people live in safety and peace for another year.

Oki looked at the bounty in his boat. Was the fruit rotten? Was the water poisoned? He stared at a sloshing gourd for a good hour before he had the courage to take a drink. Tasting its sweetness, he knew immediately it was not poisoned—it was a bribe to get him off the island quickly and permanently.

His presence was a threat to everything they believed. If he was allowed to stay, he would tell them how it was on *his* island—how God spared them from the hurricane and volcano without sacrificing a single life.

But what if the witch-doctor was right? What if *his* people were wrong?

But Oki's people performed the Ritual in their fashion and no hurricanes had set upon them. The volcano grumbled and smoked, but did not erupt or bury them in ash. Were they simply lucky? Did this mean God treated some people differently than others?

Or did it mean there was no God at all?

Oki shuddered at his blasphemy and fearfully scanned the horizon, and even as he watched, clouds began to gather. He turned his outrigger and began paddling back to the island, but it was already too late. Within minutes, a great storm tossed his boat high into the air, spilling out the baskets of fruit and dried fish. Gourds of life-giving water floated away on the roiling water. Rain pelted down on his bare back, and soon Oki felt blood trickling down his spine.

He buried his head in his hands and cried, knowing he had once again offended God with his doubts. "I'm sorry!" he sobbed into his cupped hands, tasting salt on his lips, again not knowing whether it was the ocean or his own tears.

 **SIX**

after a long and turbulent night, the sky cleared and Oki lay exhausted in the keel of his outrigger. Except for a single water gourd, his provisions had all been washed overboard, but his net still lay in a jumble in the prow, and his knife was still sheathed at his waist, so all was not lost. The sky was a brilliant blue, and the ocean was calm. A slight breeze arose, and he lifted the mast and placed it into the slot, raising the sail, which caught the wind. Oki had no idea in which direction he was moving. The sun was too far overhead to discern its path, and night was still hours away.

The wind caught the sail and as he sped along, Oki reached overboard and poured cupped handfuls of salt water onto the stinging cuts on his back. Salt water would heal him without infection, but the scars would remain with him for the rest of his life.

As he sailed, he kept his mind blank, but around nightfall he began to think again of how he had displeased God. While he remained on his own island, he saw his sins as few and minor, but now he had committed great sins on another island, offending the people, their witch-doctor, and perhaps even God himself.

But how could he offend God by telling the people what God's true will was? Was it wrong to reveal that God did not approve of the way they worshiped Him?

And yet the witch-doctor had said as much. He was the one chosen to hear God's voice, and when he flogged Oki with the spiny scepter, he was doing God's will.

Or was he?

Then, the nagging doubt surfaced again and Oki could not fight it back: Why would God reveal two different things to two different people? Wouldn't He speak the same truth to all?

Oki ducked his head as if avoiding a blow. He was ashamed to be such a doubter, but the painful flogging he'd received gave him no choice. He prayed, begging God's forgiveness and pleading for answers. When he looked up, the sun was setting in a blaze of red, the waves were still rolling under the outrigger, and the wind still shouldered its way into the tattered sail. Oki scanned the horizon for the tell-tale clouds which he had begun to associate with God's wrath at his sins, but the horizon remained flat and featureless.

Night came on and the wind did not flag, much to Oki's surprise. His outrigger sped across the dark sea, and when the North Star came out, he shook his head in wonder. He had been sailing directly for it. Yet a nagging doubt remained. If his island lay north, he would have seen it long ago, and so he knew now that he was well north of his island, moving farther away from it with each passing moment. Fear rose in his throat and tears filled his eyes. "Where are you taking me, God?" he whispered.

Well after midnight, the tiny sliver of moon appeared on the horizon, and its light was so welcoming that Oki almost turned toward it. But you could not navigate by the moon; only the North Star would lead you in a straight path. His people called the phases of the waxing moon the Seven Daughters, and each one had a name. When the full moon arrived, she was the Mother Moon, and when she waned, the Seven Grandmothers took her place, until the last grandmother died and was buried in the depths of the western sea. For two nights the world lay in deep, starlit darkness, then the first daughter, Nakiri, tentatively rose in the east. She stood now just above the horizon, slender but beautiful and bright, and Oki desperately wanted to turn his outrigger toward her, yet the tiny North Star remained motionless just above the northern horizon, and Oki forced himself to maintain his course. *Strange,* he thought. *Nakiri*

is more alluring, and she and her sisters can be seen even through the clouds of night. Yet, like a beautiful woman, she would lead me in circles. But the North Star, invisible when even a light scrim of clouds arises, is the true guide.

Oki looked at Nakiri rising in the east. *Did God send you to fool me?* he wondered. *Or merely to test me?*

seven

Dawn came and still the winds speeded Oki toward whatever distant goal—or none—which God had chosen for him. If he was to travel the seas all his days, so be it. During the long, featureless night, he found himself feeling like he was upside down. Perhaps the stars above were tiny boats in an ocean of sky, and he was a star to those travelers. What if each star was someone who had angered God and been punished to endlessly sail the seas?

What if he was actually *above* the stars and they were below? He suddenly had the urge to grab the gunwales to prevent himself from falling out of the boat and drifting upward, to land with a mighty *splash!* in the ocean of sky above him. Would he drown? Would he be rescued? Were there two islands in that sea, as there were in his? And if there were two islands, could there be three?

The thought of a third island filled his heart with hope. The wind did not abate and he grew hungry, yet he was afraid to lower his sail and cast his net for fear God would see it as a rejection of the gift of wind and take it back, leaving Oki to perish on a motionless desert of water.

His stomach howled with emptiness, yet Oki kept the sail taut and full of wind. He scanned the horizon and dared not hope for his own island again, but maybe, just maybe....

Then, toward evening, even as he watched, a dot on the horizon appeared and grew. Soon he recognized the top of an immense volcano, and the hope that he was home could not be dislodged from his heart. He let out a happy cry and steered his boat toward the island.

There was the great silver thread of waterfall cascading down from the stony heights, just like on Oki's island. Volcanic slopes were green with jungle. Soon, the blue-green of the deep ocean changed to the clear turquoise of an atoll. Two sandy arms protecting the lagoon beckoned him. Once inside its still waters, instead of the small, featureless huts of his island, Oki saw larger ones, with windows and white rocks lining curving paths running between them. A huge lodge stood in the middle of the village, twice as large as the one on Oki's island.

People on the shore saw him and left their work. A couple of youths swam out to greet him. Several women disappeared into the immense lodge, and soon a man came out wearing a feathered headdress and carrying a staff.

The witch-doctor. Oki reminded himself to mind his manners. He didn't want a repeat of his last encounter with a witch-doctor.

His boat was pulled ashore. The people gathered around him, yet they parted as the witch-doctor came forward. "You have come from across the depths of the sea!" he exclaimed.

Oki nodded.

"You had the wind at your back!" said the witch-doctor.

Oki nodded again.

"God has been with you!" cried the witch-doctor, hugging Oki tightly. But when Oki groaned in pain and pulled away, the witch-doctor examined his own hands, bloody from the cuts on Oki's back. He released Oki and slowly turned him around. The people, seeing the many open wounds on Oki's back, cried out with fear and amazement, and everyone fell to their knees and began weeping and praying.

Oki turned around, seeing the people's reaction. "I'm sorry," he said, backing away. "I'll go."

The witch-doctor took Oki's arm. "No. Tonight is the Ritual." And before Oki could speak, the witch-doctor turned and walked away. Three women came toward him, and Oki saw their eyes were not full of fear but compassion. They gently took his hands and led him up a path toward a small pool, where a waterfall spilled forth, and bid him wash himself. When he was finished, he saw a tunic of white cloth lying on the grass and put it on.

When he returned, the sun had set, and the people stood in the common area, around the great fire pit. To one side stood the villagers; to the other stood sixteen young women, their eyes bright and their long black hair glistening in the firelight.

Oki immediately looked at the witch-doctor's scepter, which was long and studded with spines, but he couldn't tell if the black tips were coated with blood. He hoped that he had at last found an island that worshiped in the true fashion, as his own people did.

The witch-doctor led the procession up the mountain. The young virgins followed the witch-doctor and seemed less terrified than the girls on the last island, yet Oki could still sense fear rising from them. Indeed, he could feel the same fear from the people who accompanied him up the path. Would the sacrifice take the life of more than just one girl? On this island, did they extend the last witch-doctor's logic even further: if a death was better than a flogging, weren't two deaths—or even more!—better yet?

Oki slowed his pace, thinking. He was prodded forward by a large man. When he looked up into the man's face, he expected to see anger or fear. What he saw in the man's eyes was unexpected: *compassion*. But compassion for whom? The victim? For Oki? For whoever else would die tonight?

Or was the look really resignation, as the man pondered his own impending death? Maybe a large number of people would be thrown into the volcano, appeasing a God that was even more demanding and implacable than the God of the last island.

At the lip of the volcano, Oki looked down into the sea of bubbling lava. The witch-doctor held his scepter, which gave Oki hope. Perhaps the witch-doctor would choose a maiden and flog her only, and then they would descend to feast and celebrate God's acceptance of the sacrifice.

But Oki couldn't help but notice that the large man remained at his side, an eye warily focused on Oki. Perhaps *he* was the sacrifice after all.

Then the witch-doctor walked slowly down the row of young girls and Oki relaxed, feeling guilty at his relief at not being chosen. The witch-doctor stopped before a tall, slender girl and nodded. The other girls ran into the arms of their mothers and fathers, sobbing with relief. The witch-doctor took the girl's hand and led her toward the precipice. She looked back longingly at her parents, who stood, holding hands and crying.

Oki took a step forward, but the large man next to him grabbed his arm, restraining him. "Don't throw her in!" shouted Oki.

With one accord, everyone turned to him, surprise on their faces.

The witch-doctor left the girl on the edge of the volcano and walked back to Oki. "What are you saying?" he asked. "That we should throw her in?"

Oki shook his head furiously. "No! *Don't* throw her in! It's wrong!"

The witch-doctor scowled at him. "Be still and watch."

Oki stood there helplessly, held tightly by the large man, watching as the witch-doctor joined the young girl on the volcano's lip. He took the girl by the wrist and turned around. "Why are we here?" he cried.

"To offer sacrifice!" shouted the people.

"Who shall we sacrifice?" cried the witch-doctor.

"Her!" said the multitude, pointing at the girl.

"Mother! Father!" she cried. "Goodbye!"

"Don't!" yelled Oki, and immediately a hand was clapped roughly over his mouth.

Then the witch-doctor did a most surprising thing. He turned away from the volcano and led the girl back a few paces, releasing his hold on her wrist. The people gathered around her and began to yell and scream at her, hurling epithets of the most vile sort.

"Harlot!" screamed a man.

"Wicked, evil monster!" shrieked an old woman.

"Unclean! Unclean!" the villagers chanted.

The girl buried her face in her hands and sobbed, falling to her knees under the onslaught of calumny and bitter accusation.

And still the insults and bitterness did not abate. They called her every horrible name, accused her of every imaginable sin, and their spit and bile rained down upon her like the burning showers of hell. She dared look up once, which only increased the volume of screams and taunts, and soon she collapsed on the ground, sobbing, her body shaking uncontrollably.

Oki watched, stunned. The large man, seeing he was no longer a threat to the Ritual, released him and joined the others in heaping scorn and insults on the poor girl, who was no longer visible beyond the heaving mass of screaming islanders.

The witch-doctor stood next to Oki, watching him carefully.

"What happens now?" asked Oki, stunned and confused.

"She will be banished," said the witch-doctor.

"Forever?"

"For a week." said the witch-doctor. "Then she will join us again. For the rest of the year she will be a reminder of how we are all unworthy of God's great gifts."

"You won't kill her?"

The witch-doctor shook his head. "No."

"And you won't flog her?"

The witch-doctor saw the blood which had soaked through the back of Oki's tunic. "What kind of barbarians would do that?" he asked.

Just then, the shouting ceased, and everyone turned their backs on the girl. Their faces were red with exertion. The witch-doctor entered the circle, took her hand, and raised her to her feet. Her eyes were wide with hurt and terror. He led her out of the circle, and as he did, the people turned again, keeping their backs to her so she could not see their faces, which, Oki noticed, were wet with tears. The witch-doctor led her down the path. Then the people turned to face the volcano, and a shallow wooden bowl was passed around. Each person guided his or her tears into the bowl. By the time it came to Oki, it was full, and Oki, without prodding, added his own tears to it.

When the witch-doctor returned, alone, he took the bowl and used his forefinger to guide his own tears into it, then gently dropped the bowl into the seething volcano.

Then the people formed a circle. Oki felt arms across his shoulders. His own hands were guided over another man's shoulders, and they all bent their heads and cried together. For a long time they stood that way, shuddering with communal sobs, until the tears were finally spent.

Oki looked around at the islanders' faces and saw a light in each one.

And he marveled.

🐚 EIGHT

It was well after midnight. The feast had been magnificent, and the dances and songs filled Oki's heart with joy and a longing for his own people and his own island.

Having seen his tears up at the volcano rim, he was accepted by the islanders as one of them, and they seated him near the witch-doctor, who asked Oki to tell them of his travels. At first he was afraid to say much, for fear of the witch-doctor's scepter, but the prodding of the people encouraged him and the pineapple wine loosened his tongue. He told them how his own people practiced the Ritual, but when he got to the part about the flogging of the virgin with the spiny scepter, the mothers covered the ears of their children and the men whispered among themselves, looking darkly at him.

Oki felt their silent condemnation and was ashamed. To cover his embarrassment, he recounted his visit to the island where they threw the young maiden into the volcano, at which point the women in the group got up quickly and took the children away. Oki was left behind, his shoulders sagging under the weight of the men's angry glares.

Tears filled Oki's eyes, and he shut them. A hand touched his forehead and he opened his eyes. He was surrounded by the men, and they gently pulled him to his feet. A hand brushed across his back and Oki heard a sob. He turned. A man was looking at blood on his fingertips. He touched his finger to his lips, tears standing in his eyes. Another man touched Oki's bloody tunic and put his finger to his lips. Soon, every man had done the same, and a drop of Oki's blood was on everyone's lips.

Then they pressed close to him and kissed him on the forehead, on the crown of his head, the back of his neck, and on his cheeks. Oki felt the moisture of their breath and felt his knees buckling. Just before passing out, he looked up and saw many kind eyes looking down at him and felt a rain of warm, salty tears on his face.

 **nine**

The next morning Oki awoke in a tiny hut. His wounds were dressed and he had been bathed. He stretched and was amazed at how little his cuts hurt him. The witch-doctor ducked inside the doorway and sat cross-legged on the ground. "Will you stay with us?" he asked.

Oki was surprised to hear his answer, for he had given it no thought at all: "No."

"I suspected as much. You are on a journey and this is not your destination."

Oki remembered being thrown off the last island. "If I wanted to, could I stay?"

"You would be welcome among us."

"But aren't you afraid of me?"

The old man smiled. "Why should we be afraid?"

Oki shrugged. "They were on the last island. I was different from them, too. I just thought . . ."

"You believe your difference is reason enough for us to cast you out."

Oki nodded.

"We are not afraid of your strange beliefs. We possess a greater truth."

"What greater truth?"

"You saw, last night," said the witch-doctor. "Our Ritual. It is superior to the Ritual your people practice."

Oki shook his head. "No, it's not."

"Tell me, Oki," said the witch-doctor, "were you being honest when you said you were horrified when they threw the young maiden into the volcano?"

Oki nodded. "It was terrible."

"It was wrong, wasn't it?"

Oki nodded.

"How do you know it was wrong?"

"Because it wasn't the way *my* people do it," said Oki, immediately feeling foolish.

"Is that the only reason it was wrong?" asked the witch-doctor, smiling slightly.

"I don't know what you mean."

"Yes, you do, Oki," said the witch-doctor. "This is a great moment for you, son. Do not fear the consequences of thinking."

Oki knew what the old man was talking about, but he *was* afraid. Thinking evil thoughts was what had got him lost upon the wide sea in the first place.

He didn't want to give God another excuse to punish him. "I'm wondering," said Oki finally, "if you believe it's permitted to question God's word or His motives." He cringed, half-expecting the old man to strike him, but when he looked up, the witch-doctor was smiling.

"Asking questions is how we learn," said the old man simply.

"Is it a sin to doubt?"

"No," said the old man. "Now answer my question: why was it wrong to cast the girl into the volcano?"

Oki looked at the old man. If he, a man chosen of God, wanted Oki to speak frankly, then it must be God's will. Oki took a deep breath. "It just felt wrong. I don't know."

The old man nodded and his smile grew. "So now *you* are a witch-doctor?"

Oki shook his head. He'd been tricked! He started to get up, but the old man gestured for him to remain seated. "Oki, as you know from your journeys, God speaks to many men. He speaks to me. He may even speak to *you*."

Oki shook his head, his mind awhirl. "But I'm not a witch-doctor! It is forbidden!"

"On *your* island," said the old man.

Oki nodded. "Only the witch-doctor hears God's voice."

"Yet you heard His voice on the other island, where they killed the girl."

Oki looked at the witch-doctor, not knowing what to say.

"You heard His voice telling you it was wrong."

"But *their* witch-doctor said *I* was wrong! He's the one who gave me these!" exclaimed Oki, pulling down his tunic to show the witch-doctor the lashes he'd received.

"*He* was wrong, Oki," said the old man.

Oki's mouth dropped open. He almost flinched, expecting a bolt of lightning to cut through the thatched roof and impale the old heretic. But nothing happened. Bird song continued in the palm trees, and the gentle mumbling of the surf continued. Oki looked around, amazed.

"Surprised?" asked the witch-doctor.

Oki nodded.

"There are many truths, Oki, greater and lesser ones. Just like the islands you've seen."

"Did you know about *my* island?"

The old man nodded.

"Where is it?"

"I don't know," said the witch-doctor.

"I want to go home," said Oki.

"You are welcome to stay here," said the witch-doctor kindly.

"I know, but I need to go."

"So God is speaking to you again," stated the old man, smiling.

"I don't know. Maybe. I'm not sure. But this place doesn't feel like home to me."

"Neither will your island," said the old man, getting to his feet. "Not anymore."

Oki looked up at him and was surprised to hear himself say, "I know."

 **TEN**

The people filled Oki's outrigger with fruit, baskets of dried fish, and gourds of fresh water. One by one, they kissed him on the eyelids as was their custom, saying, "May your eyes see truth," and bid him good bye. No one tried to dissuade him from leaving, and when the time came to cast off, they lined the shore of the lagoon.

The witch-doctor came forward. "There may be a better place for you, Oki. Maybe. We believe this is the best place there is. Won't you stay?"

Oki shook his head. "You said I could hear God's voice. There is a greater truth yet for me, I think. Out there." He turned and looked out to sea.

"But there may not be, son," said the old man. "You would be safe here, and loved. We would choose a fine woman for you, and your children would be raised in light and truth."

Oki turned back. "You yourself said there are many truths, and many islands."

The old man nodded. "But I have not seen the greater truth, Oki. Nor its island. I am afraid for you. Afraid you will be lost, when we have just barely found you, and you us."

"I know," said Oki. "I am afraid, too. But I cannot stay. I am beginning to believe this journey is not a punishment after all." He kissed the witch-doctor on the eyelids and said, "May your eyes see truth."

He could taste salt in the old man's tears.

ELEVEN

Oki was outside the lagoon before he turned back. Everyone remained on the shore, and when they saw him turn, they all shouted, "Winds! Blow!" and Oki was astonished when a moment later, a breeze lifted the hair off his forehead. He placed the mast in its slot and unfurled the triangular sail. The wind filled it and Oki felt his outrigger being pushed forward. He dipped his paddle into the water and steered the boat northward. It wasn't until he was far, far away, that he looked back again at the island, just in time to see the volcano dip below the horizon.

All that day, and the next and the next, Oki sailed north. He knew he would never see his island again, and occasionally pangs of doubt and fear entered his heart as he thought of the island he had just left, where a kind people had wanted him to stay.

He thought about the young girl who would be returning to the village in a few more days, humbled by rejection, hungry and afraid. He smiled when he thought about the reception she would receive. Washed by the other women and adorned in clean clothing, with hibiscus flowers in her hair and a lei of fragrant mimosa around her neck, she would be seated with honor at a great feast. They would sing songs about her courage. Received once more into fellowship, she would never forget her rejection and loneliness and despair, all of which was designed to teach her compassion. She would never again treat another person with indifference, for she had been rejected. She would never ridicule another again, for she had received scorn. She would never let another hunger again, for she had gone hungry.

All the days of her life, she would be an example of compassion.

Oki began to feel a pang of loneliness for the island. How he wanted to be present when the girl returned, to see the new light in her eyes and to sing songs of joy at her great courage. He wondered if anyone would ever sing a song about his courage, and was ashamed. Pride was a great sin, and wishing for a song about your courage was a perfect example of it. He ducked his head for a moment, then remembered the witch-doctor's words about hearing God's voice in his own ears. *Maybe I'm becoming a witch-doctor,* he thought, and wondered if that, too, was an example of pride. *I'm just listening for Your voice,* he amended, looking heavenward. *What would you say to me?* he wondered, feeling the wind at his back. *If you speak, I will listen.*

God didn't speak, but wind blew steadily, and Oki's outrigger whisked across the empty sea, toward a featureless horizon.

That night, as his boat sailed on, Oki dreamed of his own island. He was standing on the lip of the volcano. The witch-doctor held his scepter high and prayed. Oki didn't hear the prayer, though his eyes never left the scepter. The spines dripped with blood, which fell like hot rain onto Oki's face. He could hear the sobbing of the virgin girls as they awaited the selection, and a cold darkness filled his heart.

He awoke to rain striking his face. His sail was luffing in the changing wind. It was very dark. Kamali, Nakiri's older sister, had not yet risen. Clouds obscured the sky. He lowered the sail and stowed the mast, lashing it to the gunwales. Taking a length of rope, he carefully tied all his provisions securely inside the boat. He moved slowly, unconcerned about the rising wind and the whitecaps topping the waves. When the waves grew larger, he was ready. He tied a length of rope around his waist and nestled down onto the keel, resting his elbows on the gunwales as the waves pitched the boat to and fro. While he had been sleeping, God was preparing to speak. Oki lifted his face and closed his eyes, listening for God's voice in the thunder that split the night air.

TWELVE

The day dawned and the rain stopped, though the low clouds remained a battered blue-black, and Oki could see distant rainstorm curtains all across the gray sea. The wind died, and Oki's outrigger sat motionless on the silent, rolling ocean.

He ate a breakfast of mango and breadfruit, washed down with fresh water. Lunchtime came, and still there was no wind. He was no longer sure of his course, but Oki began to paddle anyway, though he could not tell where north was, or where the clouds ended and the sea began.

By mid-afternoon it was dark as dusk, and when the sun finally set, Oki barely noticed. Fog and mist surrounded his tiny boat, and the whole world seemed shades of gray. Sounds of distant whale song drifted across the still water, mournful and aching, and Oki felt terribly alone and lonely. He took a couple of swigs of sweet pineapple wine, but dared not risk getting drunk. Out here, in the midst of the ocean, things could change very quickly, and he would need all his faculties to deal with them.

Toward midnight, the clouds thinned enough to see the stars, pale and tiny, nothing like the sparkling beacons he had imagined as tiny boats on the upside-down world where he was a guiding star to a lonely voyager. The thought of people in all those tiny boats on that immense, far away ocean filled him with despair and he wept, his shoulders shaking with the effort. His sobs continued long after his tears had stopped, and he realized he would die out here on the empty ocean. He had left the last, best island in the world—there was no other island, no greater truth, and he was a fool.

A fool that would perish of thirst on an ocean of water.

He dipped his hand into the water and poured the salt water onto the cuts on his back. It stung, and he was once again reminded of how small and unimportant his life must be. God, who knew everything and everyone, knew about Oki as well.

He just didn't care.

 # THIRTEEN

Seven days and nights passed, and the wind did not blow. Oki rationed his food and cast his net into the still water, but caught no fish. He had never seen the sea so quiet. The surface was like a great mirror, reflecting the tall, billowing clouds that passed overhead, their bottoms gray, heavy with rain, but they did not pause to give Oki a drink, but continued on to the east, messengers carrying a life gift not intended for disobedient fishermen.

His food ran out on the fifth day. He dared not drink the last swallow of water in the gourd. At noon, he gave up paddling because he could not tell if he was making any progress. The skies were a high, flat gray, and the sun was invisible.

When night fell, Oki hoped the sky would clear and the stars would come out, but the sky remained cloudy. He leaned back in the keel of the boat, stretched out his tired legs, and tried to sleep. But sleep would not come, and the emptiness and quiet of the ocean soon filled his ears with loneliness, and he felt himself crying once again, though without tears.

I'll die out here, he thought. *I should have stayed with them.* His mind returned to the previous island. By now, the young virgin had returned from exile, and they were feasting in her honor. The thought of food and drink parched his throat and he raised the gourd. It was nearly empty; only one mouthful of water sloshed inside. But as his lips touched the opening, he stopped, hearing something.

He turned and looked at the empty, dark ocean behind him. Squinting, he thought he saw black shapes moving above, below, and upon the face of the dark water, coming toward him. He stoppered the gourd and lifted his paddle in defense, his eyes scanning the blackness. He half expected a great sea monster to rear out of the ocean and devour his tiny outrigger in one huge bite. He shook his head. He was delirious. Water would cure that. He opened the gourd again and studied the spout. He dared not drink it. It was the last, final hope for a successful end to his journey. If he drank it now, he knew he would perish out here on the ocean. While there was still hope, he would refrain. Fighting the urge to take a drink, he pushed the cork into the opening and promised himself that he would not take that drink until he stood on the shore of the Last Island.

As he peered into the darkness, he imagined the Last Island. It would be bigger than the others— greater truth always was—and would have a huge volcano reaching high into the sky. There would be a Ritual on the volcano's lip, but Oki could not imagine how it would unfold. He was certain they would not kill anyone, or flog anyone, or even shame anyone.

But then how would they appease God? How would they assuage His anger and secure His protection against the hurricanes and eruptions? There must be some sort of sacrifice, but Oki could not fathom what it might be.

Then he heard something, a distant high-pitched chattering. He strained to see through the mist surrounding him. And there, just under the surface of the water, an immense dark, arrow-shaped form moved slowly toward him. Oki cocked his paddle, terrified. Was this the sea monster he'd imagined, its hungry mouth already open, huge, sharp teeth ready for the taste of human flesh?

Oki cinched the rope around his waist and watched the black form approach. He grasped the paddle tightly and waited, his heart trip-hammering in his throat. Then the monster's back broke the water in a dozen places, leaving white trails behind what looked like raised scales. It moved inexorably forward, and was now within a stone's throw of his outrigger. He steeled himself for impact.

Suddenly the great black shape broke apart and something long and smooth leapt from the water right in front of him. Just before it slipped back into the placid water, Oki caught a glimpse of a great, sad eye. On the other side of his boat, another form cleared the water, and Oki saw a long strip of teeth, like tiny bleached stones, and another eye surveyed him for an instant before the shape nosed back into the water.

Oki smiled. Dolphins! A school of them—perhaps twenty or more—was his feared monster! Their chattering was the gentle speech of the Friendly Fish, as his people called them. More of them leapt free from the water, shining, and slipping back in as smoothly as they left it. Many others slipped under the boat, rocking it, making Oki drop his paddle and grab the gunwales to avoid being thrown overboard.

He expected them to continue past him, but the leaders turned and swam back. They squeaked to him joyfully. *Come and play! Come and play!* they seemed to be saying, and Oki almost jumped into the water right then, to join them.

When he was a boy, occasionally a dolphin would
venture into the warm, shallow waters of the lagoon.
The children would hold out morsels of fresh fish,
and when the dolphin came near, they would grab
its smooth dorsal fin for a ride. At first, the dolphin
would be alarmed, and would do its best to shed
the laughing child, but once dislodged, the child
would toss a bit of fish to the dolphin. Dolphins are
smart, and soon learned that a short ride across the
lagoon was a small price to pay for a tender morsel
of food.

Oki had been one of those children, and wished
he had a piece of fish right now to give his visitors,
but he had none. And out here, in the middle of the
ocean, he dared not join them in the water. They
might mistake him for a predator, or leave him
entirely as quickly as they came, and he wanted that
least of all.

He was watching the cavorting dolphins, when
something hit the bow of his outrigger. He sat down,
grabbing the gunwales, looking around. Perhaps
there was a sea monster after all. Then he saw the
culprit: the dolphin which had struck the boat glided

under it and circled back. Oki lost sight of it, but felt it hit the boat again, in the exact same place—the port bow. The boat rocked crazily, and the dolphin disappeared. A few more blows like that and the outrigger's hull would be breached, and Oki would drown. He raised his paddle, ready to hit the dolphin when it circled back. He saw it an instant before it hit the boat the third time, and flailed ineffectively at it. And as he watched it swim under the outrigger, another blow came. Oki whirled around and saw another dolphin disappear. Then another appeared out of the darkness, hit the boat with its snout, and though Oki swung his paddle as hard as he could, he was simply not fast enough. A procession of dolphins was bent on destroying his boat. Oki's heart climbed up into his throat.

His delight at the dolphins' visit sizzled away into hot anger. They were trying to kill him! He swung the paddle, barely missing a dolphin as it nudged the boat. When the next dolphin raised its snout, Oki stabbed at it with the paddle, striking the hump between its eyes. Oki was glad when he saw it surface on the other side of his boat, listing to one side, blood pouring out of a deep gash. But then the outrigger was hit three times in quick succession, and Oki fell overboard, flailing, into the cold water.

Gasping for breath, Oki surfaced. He found himself in the midst of the dolphins, and the blood in the water agitated them. He was hit several times with hard, pointy snouts. He swallowed water, got into a coughing fit, and when he regained his senses, he couldn't see his outrigger in the darkness. Luckily, he remembered the rope at his waist. He began reeling himself in, knowing he was tethered to the boat, and if he survived the dolphins' anger, he might yet get back aboard. A dolphin nipped at his foot and he kicked, striking something soft. Another butted him in the back, causing him to cry out in pain. Now his own blood mingled with the water, and all around him, the dolphins chattered excitedly. When he finally grasped the outrigger, still blind in the darkness, the boat was still being pushed to the right by a succession of dolphins. He hauled himself back on board, felt the boat being struck again, and felt around in the darkness for the paddle. It was gone. Another dolphin hit the boat and Oki screamed, "Stop it!"

Then, just as quickly as they began, the dolphins stopped butting the boat. They circled the outrigger a couple of times, a dozen pale eyes surveying him placidly, then vanished, disappearing into the sea depths.

And before he could take another breath, the wind began to blow. Oki scrambled to upright the mast and hoist the sail. The craft took off across the water at a speedy clip. It was pitch black, both before and behind, but within minutes, the clouds had lifted and the stars shone brightly. And directly off the bow was the North Star, twinkling in the dark sky. On the eastern horizon, the full Mother Moon made her long-anticipated appearance.

Within an hour, the clouds were a memory and Mother Moon rode high in the sky, casting a silver light across the expanse of ocean. The wind pushed Oki's outrigger before it with such great command that he gave up dragging a foot to steer, but simply put himself in its hands. The sail was full and the course did not vary from true north as the outrigger skimmed the waves.

Oki lay back in the keel. The crisp, clear night, the North Star, and Mother Moon, created an unearthly tableau. He leaned over the side and saw, to his utter amazement, deep beneath him in the clear water, the dolphins, swimming along with him, matching his prodigious speed. Now and then one would draw close to the boat and gently nudge it before disappearing again into the darkness below. Oki looked at the North Star directly before him and tears filled his eyes. In the doldrums, the dolphins, seeing his plight, had been nudging his outrigger to true north, and he had killed one of them! And even now, they were still guiding his course.

Oki buried his head in his hands and cried, shedding as many tears as there was fresh water sloshing in the gourd. His outrigger sped along the surface of the dark sea, nudged to the proper course by his fellow travelers, the dolphins, and overseen by the majesty of Mother Moon, who sailed high in the sky and saw all.

FOURTeen

morning came and still the boat raced on, guided by the dolphins. Each time one surfaced, Oki looked to see if it was the one he'd struck with the oar. It never appeared, and Oki felt sick with regret at his actions of the night before.

The near-empty gourd sloshed at his feet. Oki's lips grew parched, and he found himself staring at the gourd for minutes on end, licking his lips. But the presence of the dolphins reminded him he was on no ordinary journey. He had vowed to not drink the water until he stood on the shore of the Last Island and he knew he must not break that promise.

Tall, fluffy cumulus clouds moved west to east, but the wind in Oki's sails still pushed his boat northward. He wondered how that could be, then thought, *It's not the wind; it's the breath of God.*

And then a shaft of sunlight lit the distance and Oki jumped to his feet. The cone of a great volcano rose above green mountain shoulders. Oki scanned the water. It was deep green, not the turquoise surrounding most islands. He shook his head in wonder. It must be an immense island, to be so big at this great a distance, yet he could make out many details. A dozen waterfalls cascaded from its volcanic heights.

When the reef finally skimmed silently under his outrigger, Oki noticed the dolphins had disappeared. He looked astern and whispered his thanks, promising he would never again injure one of their number for any reason.

Oki turned back. The outstretched arms of a great lagoon beckoned him. On the shore stood a huge, multi-storied lodge. Dozens of huts surrounded it, and boats of all shapes and sizes were pulled up on the sandy beach. A distant horn blew, and people looked up from their labors. Seeing him enter the lagoon, they began to gather on the shore. Oki lowered his sail and disengaged the mast. From the immense lodge came a procession, led by a man holding a tall, smooth staff.

As Oki reached the shore, the witch-doctor said, "Welcome, traveler. We have been waiting for you."

 # FIFTeen

They stood around the bonfire, which threw sparks into the cool night air. Every one was gathered, and Oki was among them. After he had eaten and bathed, an old woman gave him a new tunic. When he turned his back to put it on, he looked back over his shoulder to see what her reaction would be. She simply nodded and left.

Oki was surprised: he'd expected more of a reaction. But the people, though they were friendly, were not inquisitive. No one asked him where he had come from. No one asked him where he was going. And no one asked him how he got the scars.

And now he stood with the people, surrounding the fire. They were chanting in a strange tongue, their voices rising and falling, their eyes shut. Oki did not understand the words, but they nevertheless slipped effortlessly into his mind and before long, his eyes were closed and he was chanting as if he'd known the words all his life. And when the last refrain died, Oki was disappointed. He opened his eyes.

He stood alone on one side of the bonfire. The entire village faced him across the dancing flames, and all were watching him. Oki looked around for the virgins, who should have been standing where he stood. There were a number of young maidens with their families across from him, but he alone stood on this side of the fire pit.

Oki looked down and noticed that his tunic was a blinding white, the color of sacrifice. He wanted to run, but where would he go? He didn't know this island and they would soon catch him. So he stood his ground and waited. The witch-doctor began making his way around the fire pit. When he stood before Oki, he said, "The Ritual awaits."

Devoid of hope, Oki nodded.

The old man gripped Oki's wrist, and Oki, so recently delivered from the ocean's grasp, had never felt death hold him so tightly before, even when he languished in the doldrums those seven days. It was useless to resist. The people formed a line behind them and the witch-doctor took the first step toward the volcano. As he climbed the path, Oki knew why they had been so glad to see him this afternoon.

Had he come all this way, only to be thrown into the volcano? Or would he be flogged with a spiny scepter, like on his own island? He looked behind him. The people's faces were impassive, turned inward. No one held a terrifying, blood-encrusted scepter, though there were suspicious bulges under many tunics. Oki wondered if they hid knives there, to tear him apart on the volcano precipice.

Oki gulped and shook the image away. Maybe they would simply hurl insults at him and cast him out, to receive him again within a week, the guest of honor at their feast. But then he recalled that he had not been present when the girl came back. Maybe they had lied to him about receiving her again. Maybe the young girl had been cast out forever, never to return. And maybe that would be Oki's fate tonight.

Or maybe his fate would be worse. For each island, though their Rituals contained many similar elements, had its own twist on the sacrifice itself. Oki hoped that the Ritual on this island was a greater truth than on the last, but he could not imagine what it might be. He was reminded of what the witch-doctor on the second island said, just before they cast him out: "Death is a greater sacrifice than a mere flogging—wouldn't it please God more?"

If that was so, there must be a sacrifice even greater than death. Oki shivered, unable to imagine what it might be. He looked up and saw the smoking summit, the low-lying clouds burnished red from the volcano's fiery core. The stones under his feet shook. Oki knew his entire island could easily fit inside the maw of this giant volcanic monster, and still the fire and smoke and thunderous roar was a trifle compared to his fear of the impending sacrifice.

He wished to be back out on the stormy ocean, hurled between mountain-sized swells, being pelted with cold rain. He wished he was starving on the doldrums, his tongue swollen from lack of water. He wished for the spiny scepter thudding against his bare back. He wished for rejection and eternal exile. He even wished for immolation, so long as it came quick.

He wished to be anywhere but here.

 **SIXTEEN**

s they approached the summit, Oki's hands shook more than the ground under his feet. The witch-doctor would not let him go, but held his wrist tightly. Oki looked for compassion on the old man's face, but only a steely resolve lodged among the crags and lines there.

Oki looked back at the islanders. On his island, the people turned away when the victim was flogged bloody, unable to bear it. On the second island, they watched in grim fascination as the girl was hurled into the fiery pit. On the third island, the people cried tears of compassion. But here, on the Last Island, they walked up the path as if in a dream, apparently disconnected from the unfolding event, each lost in his or her own thoughts.

And now they stood on the precipice which overhung the volcano's fiery throat. Far below, Oki saw the bubbling cauldron. Heat rose in great waves, singing the hairs on his eyebrows and scalding his forehead, which was sheened with fearful sweat.

The witch-doctor left Oki on the precipice and turned back to the people. "Why are we here?" he shouted, raising his smooth staff.

"To offer sacrifice!" cried the people.

"Who shall we sacrifice?"

"Him!" they shouted, pointing at Oki, who felt his knees trembling, certain he would pitch himself into the volcano of his own accord in another moment.

The witch-doctor turned and faced Oki. To Oki's surprise, he was holding the gourd from Oki's outrigger. He sloshed it near his ear, then gave it to Oki. Oki looked at the gourd, puzzled. His excitement at arriving on the Last Island had been so great that he'd forgotten to drink the last mouthful of water when he stood on the white beach. It seemed like days ago now.

"What is this for?" Oki shouted above the volcano's roar.

"Will you keep your promise?" shouted the witch-doctor.

"What promise?"

"The promise we all made." Then the witch-doctor slid his tunic off his skinny shoulders and turned around. His back was covered with row upon row of white, knotted scars, like frayed ropes just under the skin's surface. He looked over his shoulder at Oki, waiting.

Oki stared in dumb astonishment.

The witch-doctor nodded at the islanders. With one accord, they turned and lowered their tunics. Every person had a criss-crossing of scars across their backs.

"Where did you get those scars?" asked Oki, finding his voice.

"From the other islands," said the old man.

"You were there, too?"

The people nodded, and Oki unraveled the emotions on their faces. It was not compassion, it was not sympathy, nor was it concern for a person who is suffering. No. Those dark faces, rimmed by black hair, showed *empathy*. They had been where Oki had been. They, too, had crossed the great ocean, risking everything. And each had arrived here and stood where Oki stood now. He nodded at the witch-doctor. "What should I do?"

"Make the sacrifice," said the witch-doctor.

Oki held the gourd up. "Is this it?"

The old man said, "You promised to drink the last mouthful when you arrived on the Last Island. Do you believe you are there?"

Oki looked at the gourd, puzzled. Why was he standing on the edge of a volcano holding this gourd, when, if they wanted him to drink from it, they could have given it to him down on the beach, in the lagoon? Something was not right.

"I'm not sure," ventured Oki.

"Why?" asked the witch-doctor.

Oki felt the peril of his position. If the old man swung his staff, he could easily knock Oki off the precipice and into the fiery pit. They would have their sacrifice after all. He didn't want to antagonize the old man, but something was amiss. "I don't know!"

"Is this the Last Island?" pressed the witch-doctor.

"I'm not sure!"

The old man stared at him. Oki knew everything hinged on what he would say next. They could easily kill him. He was weak from his journey, and his mind was empty of ideas. He had no more questions, no more reason to disagree or agree. He was standing on a cliff high above a volcano and his life was ending. Only the truth would go with him into the next world.

"No!" he shouted, suddenly filled with rage. "This is *not* the Last Island!" He glared at the witch-doctor.

The witch-doctor pursed his lips and looked intently at Oki, then turned back to the people. Each of them came forward, reaching inside his or her tunic, producing a small gourd or a clay jug or a hollowed out coconut. The vessels were placed at Oki's feet reverently, like holy relics. Then the witch-doctor withdrew a dried up water skin from inside his tunic and sat it with the others.

"We were all lost at sea, as you were," he said. "We all had one swallow of water left, as you did. We all promised to drink it on the shore of the Last Island, as you have."

"But this is not the Last Island!" shouted Oki.

The old man nodded.

"Then what am I supposed to sacrifice?" asked Oki. "This?" He held up his gourd.

The witch-doctor produced a shallow wooden bowl, much like the tear-catcher from the third island. He gave Oki the bowl. "Your fear."

"My fear?"

"You have crossed the empty ocean," said the witch-doctor. "You faced the trials and learned to trust your own mind, not that of any witch-doctor. You knew killing the girl was wrong, so you left the second island. You could not stay on the third island, for it was a dead place, full of compassion but empty of growth. You braved the doldrum seas and received the dolphin guides, who led you here. You have no more need for fear."

"Will I journey onto the sea again?"

The old man shrugged. "Perhaps. But you will do it without fear. Fear must be left here, on this island."

Oki turned and faced the volcanic holocaust. He clutched the bowl tightly in both hands and closed his eyes. *God,* he prayed, *can I live without my fear? What shall I use in its place?*

Oki listened. Below him, the volcano shrieked, red flames licking upward, but a tiny voice came to him across the expanse of thunder and violence. *I will give you love and it will fill you up. You will never be empty again.*

Oki looked into the bowl and poured his fear into it. The hatred, the jealousy, the greed—which were all forms of fear—went into the bowl. The hunger for approval, the desire to be loved, the loneliness—which were all forms of fear—went into the bowl. The pride of accomplishment, the longing for recognition, the cataloging of injuries—which were all forms of fear—went into the bowl. He staggered under its dark weight, and he tipped it toward the cauldron below. He was engulfed in a blast of steam and reeled backwards, losing his grip in the bowl, which bounced on the craggy rock, then fell into the volcano.

Oki stumbled back from the edge and fell to the ground. Just before he passed out, he looked up into the face of the witch-doctor and wondered, *Am I still afraid?*

seventeen

Oki awoke the next morning in a small hut. Just inside the door was a tortoise shell of ripe fruit, freshly broiled fish, and sweet banana bread. He ate the food and inhaled the fresh morning air. Outside, he heard voices. He poked his head out of the hut and saw an old woman and an old man running along the sand, playing tag, laughing. It was children's laughter, and Oki smiled. Old people, playing like children, even *sounding* like children.

He walked out of the hut and sat on a split log near the fire pit. The coals of last night's fire smouldered beneath a gray blanket of ash. The witch-doctor appeared and sat next to Oki. For a long time they stared into the coals, saying nothing. Finally, the witch-doctor asked, "How long will you stay with us?"

Oki was surprised at the question. "Do I have to go?"

"Of course not, but water still sloshes in your gourd."

"I don't understand."

The witch-doctor reached under his tunic and produced the leather waterskin he'd shown Oki the night before. "It is long since dried up," he said ruefully.

"Why don't you fill it?"

"Because I am not making that journey."

"Why not?"

"I am too old."

Oki watched the two old people frolicking near the shore. He nodded at them. "No one is old here."

"Hold on to that thought," said the witch-doctor.

Oki looked at the old man. "Do you *want* to go?"

"Sometimes. Especially when a new arrival comes. Especially then."

"Then why don't you?" said Oki. "You said this is not the Last Island,"

"You're right. It's not."

"Are you afraid to leave?"

The old man laughed. "No. I just don't *want* to."

Oki nodded, understanding. "Because you're the witch-doctor."

"It's not that," said the witch-doctor. "The position rotates. Everyone has their turn. No one is special or chosen to lead. All are equal, men and women, old and young. No. What I would give up is the fellowship of my friends. They are my family."

"But perhaps a greater family awaits you on the Last Island," said Oki.

"That may be true," said the old man. "But I have traveled far enough, my young friend. I am tired. I will stay here."

"But why?" enthused Oki. "We're so very close! I can feel it! There is another, greater island waiting for us."

"Just one?"

"I don't know," said Oki. "Maybe, maybe not. It doesn't matter. We're *supposed* to make this journey—I see that now. I saw it last night, up on the volcano. I'm not afraid, and I don't care what happens to my body! God will set the North Star ablaze! He will send Mother Moon to light the night! He will send dolphins to guide me in the darkness when the stars are obscured! And He will fill my gourd with water!"

The old man picked up Oki's gourd and smiled. "I will help you pack your outrigger."

EIGHTEEN

Oki paddled across the lagoon. Behind him, the witch-doctor held his staff high in farewell. Oki waved back and turned to survey his outrigger. He had left his fishing net on the shore, along with his knife. No baskets of dried fish or fresh fruit rocked in the keel. No stoppered coconuts or full-to-bursting water skins lay next to the baskets. No provisions whatsoever, except for a single gourd with a cork stopper. Oki lifted the gourd to his ear. Inside, the last mouthful of water still sloshed, waiting for the day when he would set foot on the Last Island.

The one provision he'd taken from the island was a paddle, and it cut the water cleanly. Oki shrugged off his tunic, exposing his scarred back to the sun, and splashed salt water on the wounds. The salt water would heal them without infection. Salt water healed all wounds without infection.

Oki slotted the mast into place, then raised the sail. The noonday sun made a triangular shadow on the clear water of the lagoon. Hundreds of colorful fish swam underneath the outrigger. He looked back and heard the people on shore call, "Wind! Blow!" and felt a shiver of excitement as the wind rose behind him, catching the sail, billowing it out before the boat. Soon the outrigger was running with the wind, the sail rope taut in Oki's hand, his other holding the paddle steady in the water, steering the boat. The sun felt good on his back, and his stomach was full. Last night they had a small feast for him. There was singing and delicious food, and friendship flowed like pineapple wine as they talked about the Journey, and they sang the song he'd first heard around the bonfire the night before. He hummed its infectious melody now as his outrigger raced along the tops of the waves, breaking clear of the sandy arms encircling the placid lagoon.

For several hours he raced northward, the great island shrinking into the distance behind him, until it disappeared below the curve of ocean. To his left, the sun was sinking toward a bank of clouds hugging the horizon. To his right, Makala, the first of the Grandmother Moons, would rise in a few hours, and she would light his way tonight.

Below him coursed unseen schools of dolphins, his guides and friends, who would nudge him toward the Next Island. He'd given up thinking of a Last Island, for he knew that if there were two islands, there were three. If there were three, there were four, and if there were four...

Nervousness skittered around in his heart, and for an instant he mistook it for fear. But then he realized it was anticipation, a most welcome fellow traveler.

And when the sun slid down to meet the clouds in a glorious burst of yellow and orange and crimson and finally a deep, radiant purple, he knew he had another companion riding the waves with him. Oki waited for the North Star to appear and when it did, glimmering out of the blue-black darkness, he smiled.

"Welcome, my God, my friend," he whispered into the warm breeze. "Is this *your* journey, too?"